Prayers

for a

Friend

Much love,
Susie

Vernet Clemons Nettles, Ed.D.

To Betty Roscoe,
Your friendship is
special! Continue
to be blessed!
always
Vernet
Aug 4, 2023

BK
ROYSTON
Publishing

BK Royston Publishing
www.bkroystonpublishing.com
bkroystonpublishing@gmail.com

@ Copyright – 2021

Scripture from The Holy Bible, New King James
Version, Copyright© 1982 Thomas Nelson.

New Living Translation (NLT) *Holy Bible*, New Living
Translation, copyright © 1996, 2004, 2015 by
Tyndale House Foundation. Used by permission of
Tyndale House Publishers, Inc., Carol Stream, Illinois
60188. All rights reserved.

Cover Design: Elite Book Covers
Back Cover Photographer: Key Moments Media, LLC-
Kellee Forte, Montgomery, AL

ISBN: 978-1-955063-30-2

Printed in the United States

Table of Contents

Acknowledgements

This prayer journey is first dedicated to *My Almighty and Most Gracious Father God,* who has sustained me and showed out – once again.

To *my village* who didn't know I was struggling but obeyed the call of God to text or call and say, "Hey Nettles lady. You ok?" or Hey, Muffin, you alright?"

To *my daughter,* who teaches me unconditional love.

To *my family,* who reads all the words that I pray and share. And respond because they love me: "Oh, that was really good." LOLOL

To Julia, my friend and publisher – simply amazing. And, Brian is my bonus.

Most of this year (2021) I've been in a stuck. I am blessed that the fog is lifting and grateful to these people and more who hung in with me – whether they knew or not. It's not the whining – it's the love.

Thank you all for the Love.

Amen

The Flower

The *African Violet* represents spiritual wisdom, faithfulness, and humility.

https://www.kremp.com/etymology-and-symbolism-of-50-flowers

"Now this is the confidence that we have in Him, that if we ask anything according to His will, He hears us. And if we know that He hears us, whatever we ask, we know that we have the petitions that we have asked of Him."

I John 5:14-15 NKJV

Reading by the numbers

There are two numbers that are prominent in this prayer journey. The numbers **10** and **40**. When this happens in my books, it is rarely deliberate. The number count shows itself as I am completing the process and I am ALWAYS amazed, then grateful.

- The **number 10** signifies completion and testimony. There are 10 scriptures strategically placed throughout this journey to remind us to hear the heart of God. It is our testimony.

- The **number 40** signifies a period of testing or trial. Many of these prayers were written when my family or friends were facing personal struggles. I am always blessed when He delivers the words for me to share then; and I am humbled that He selected 40 for me to share now.

Amen

Introduction

Over the years I have texted prayers to my friends, family, colleagues and others as I have been inspired - for comfort, peace, encouragement, or just because.

This is a compilation of prayers that I hope have been of comfort to those who received them. It is my prayer that those who are reading them now will be blessed.

Read, Pray, Share

Cover us

Heavenly Father, thank you for all things. It is my prayer that you cover us in your keeping grace. Whether they are physical, spiritual, or emotional challenges we shall face, we seek your grace. We may not know, acknowledge, or speak aloud our concerns but we place them in your hands. For these blessings and your quieting of spirit we pray, in Jesus' name.

Amen.

"Be anxious for nothing, but in everything by prayer and supplication, with thanksgiving, let your requests be made known to God; and the peace of God, which surpasses all understanding, will guard your hearts and minds through Christ Jesus."

Philippians 4:6-7 NKJV

Prayer of Thankfulness

Heavenly Father, thank you for all things - for each opportunity to talk with you. Thank you for waking us this morning to have another opportunity to love you and love each other. Thank you for sound minds, help us to use our thoughts and abilities to increase your kingdom and serve each other. Thank you for each other, for the friends and family you have placed in our lives to walk with us in this journey. Grant us peace as you send your Spirit to be with us. In Jesus' name we pray and praise. Thank you, Lord.

Amen.

_____

_____

_____

_____

_____

_____

_____

_____

_____

_____

Prayer of Praise

Heavenly Father, thank you. We stand in awe of your majesty and of your presence in our lives. We are standing in celebration, and we are grateful for all that you have done for our family and our extended families. Father, we continue to pray that you will lift _____ as she begins this chapter as a _____, and that she will be able to stand for right, stand in integrity, and always stand in you. In Jesus' name we pray, we celebrate, we praise, and we say thank you.

Amen.

Pray, Journal, Reflect

_____

_____

_____

_____

_____

_____

_____

_____

_____

_____

Prayer for my Daughter

Heavenly Father, thank you for all things. Father, thank you for your hedge of protection around _____. Thank you for assuring her that she is your child. Thank you for revealing to her who is against her and who is for her. Father, continue to grant her discernment and courage, so that she hears and recognizes your still small voice in her heart above all others. Please, please, continue to strengthen her along this journey. Remind her that she has value, and she is valued. Thank you for all that you have done and all that you will do in her life. In Jesus' name we pray and praise.

Amen.

Pray, Journal, Reflect

Prayer for Parents

Gracious Father, we thank you for our parents. Thank you for choosing them to be our loving earthly examples. Thank you for the lessons and the love they poured into us. Thank you for the strength and courage that they modeled so that we could follow in defined footsteps. Thank you also for their love of you, Lord, as they taught us to know you, to love you, and to depend upon your grace. Thank you, Father, for these thy gifts. In Jesus' name we praise and pray.

Amen.

Pray, Journal, Reflect

_____

_____

_____

_____

_____

_____

_____

_____

_____

_____

Prayer for a Caregiver

Heavenly Father, we thank you. We ask for strength, Lord, to do what we know is the right thing - a means to provide the best care for _____. Guide us so that we know that you are in this decision. Help _____ to understand that we love her. And help us to know that she loves us too. This is so difficult for us all. Thank you for your grace and the loving comfort of your arms. Keep us, Father, we depend on you today. For these and other blessings we pray.

Amen.

_____

_____

_____

_____

_____

_____

_____

_____

_____

_____

_____

Prayer of Thanksgiving

Heavenly Father, thank you for all things. Father, thank you for dwelling in my heart and in my spirit, for guiding me, for teaching me - so that whatever I do is done to your glory and in the name of Christ Jesus. We love you, Lord, and want your spirit to overflow in us so that others may see and know your glory. In Jesus' name we pray.

Amen.

"God has given each of you a gift from his great variety of spiritual gifts. Use them well to serve one another."

1 Peter 4:10 NLT

Prayer before an Interview

Heavenly Father, we pray today that you calm my nerves and my fears. Guide my mind and my heart so that my answers are clear, direct, and representative of the task ahead. You have poured into me a wealth of knowledge and love for your children. Please, Lord, allow that to rise to the surface and be apparent. But most important, let your will be done. We pray for a successful interview and that whatever the results, that you are pleased. In Jesus' name we pray and say thank you.

Amen.

Pray, Journal, Reflect

_____

_____

_____

_____

_____

_____

_____

_____

_____

_____

Prayer on the Job

My Lord, My God, calm _____ *'s spirit. Help* _____ *to be strong and remember that you are our source. Help* _____ *to continue to work in this environment and not be changed or singed by all that swirls around* _____. *Father, thank you for being our source and reminding us that we are to be of service for your kingdom. In Jesus' name we pray and praise you for the journey. Thank you, Lord.*

Amen.

Pray, Journal, Reflect

_____

_____

_____

_____

_____

_____

_____

_____

_____

_____

Prayer for Covering

Heavenly Father, we thank you for all things. We pray today for your grace. We seek truth, Father, and honesty of circumstances. Father, we ask that daggers formed do not meet their target and that your truth and glory is evident. Thank you, Father. For this and other blessings we do pray.

Amen.

Pray, Journal, Reflect

_____

_____

_____

_____

_____

_____

_____

_____

_____

_____

Prayer for our Gifts

Good morning, Lord, and thank you for all things - for each talent and gift that you have given me. Father, we pray for revelation of our purpose. Help us to see the true gifts and talents you have blessed us with. Help us to make room in our lives for us to understand what they are and to share them with others. Remind us that each time we share what we know how to do or what we have with others we are sharing a part of you. Calm our hearts and comfort our souls. We need to hear from you. In Jesus' name we pray and praise your name.

Amen.

"But certainly God has heard me; He has attended to the voice of my prayer. Blessed be God, Who has not turned away my prayer, Nor His mercy from me!"

Psalms 66:19-20 NKJV

Prayer of Comfort – for our Grief

Heavenly Father, we ask for strength; we ask for courage; we ask for healing of our broken hearts for you have called our loved one home. We do not understand why, but we agree that you are a God of Love and of Hope and as we travel this path of grief you will not leave us alone. Welcome our loved one into your bosom we pray. Grant _____ peace from suffering. Grant us the peace of Your Assurance. We thank you for our time together and look forward to the reunion in Your home. In Jesus' name we pray.

Amen.

Pray, Journal, Reflect

_____

_____

_____

_____

_____

_____

_____

_____

_____

_____

Prayer of Comfort – Loss of a Father

Precious Lord, take our hands this day as we lay our Father to rest. Remind us that You are the Ultimate Father, and you are with us during this difficult place. Grant us strength for the day, comfort in our spirit, peace in our hearts, and the joy of precious memories. Thank you, Father, for the life and love of our dad. He is missed. For these and many other blessings we need today, we pray and trust you, Lord.

Amen.

Pray, Journal, Reflect

Prayer of Comfort – Loss of a Father

Heavenly Father, thank you for all things - for your comfort even as you dispense your will. Help us to accept the unexpected passing of our father, husband, grandfather, _____. Remind us of the years of love we have had and that in time we will see him again. Thank you for his presence in our lives and for the time we had. Walk with us during this time; we need you. Let each tear be one of fond memories and healing. We thank you for all things and the continuous comfort of your loving arms. In Jesus' name we pray and say thank you.

Amen.

Pray, Journal, Reflect

_____

_____

_____

_____

_____

_____

_____

_____

_____

_____

Prayer of Comfort – Loss of a Mother

Heavenly Father, thank you for all things. Father, we come today seeking your comfort. We thank you for the years of love and joy of our mother. We thank you for a life well lived. We know that she now sits with you and she is well. We seek prayers as we send her physically to rest, but spiritually awakened with you. In Jesus' name we pray and praise.

Amen*.*

Pray, Journal, Reflect

_____

_____

_____

_____

_____

_____

_____

_____

_____

_____

Prayer of Comfort – Loss of a Mother

Gracious Father, heal my wounded heart. Father, thank you for the years that I cared for my mother and thank you for the years that she cared for me. She was my best friend. And as I watched her grow more and more ill, I saw her faith in you never waiver. Thank you for the lesson in her life. Father, thank you for bringing her to her heavenly home, no longer in pain, no longer in need. She has all she needs in you. Heal my heart, Lord. Help me to be all that she wanted and all that you have planned for my life. In Jesus' name I pray and rest in your arms.

Amen.

Pray, Journal, Reflect

_____

_____

_____

_____

_____

_____

_____

_____

_____

_____

Prayer of Comfort – Loss of a Husband

Heavenly Father, we come to you with bowed heads and humble hearts. We ask for your comfort, Father, as we lay our loved one to his earthly rest. Our hearts are sad, and we miss him; but we are comforted by your mercy on us in our grief and on our loved one who is now released from pain. Grant him rest. Father, we ask for your arms of strength and courage to continue on. Comfort us, strengthen us, and keep us as only you can - today, tomorrow, and the days to come. Our hearts are sad, but joyous as we take comfort in your perfect peace. In Jesus' name we pray and say thank you.

Amen.

Pray, Journal, Reflect

_____

_____

_____

_____

_____

_____

_____

_____

_____

_____

_____

Prayer of Comfort – Loss of a Wife

Father God, give _____ strength for this day - moment by moment. In his sorrow, remind him of your love - in the little things - moment by moment. Help him draw strength from you, so that he can be strong for his children, who grieve as well. Father, we need you now in this moment and the next. We love you; we thank you; we praise you for this moment - moment by moment. In Jesus' name we pray.

Amen.

Pray, Journal, Reflect

_____

_____

_____

_____

_____

_____

_____

_____

_____

_____

Vernet Clemons Nettles, Ed.D. |34

Prayer of Comfort - Loss of a Son

My Lord, My God, my heart is broken. Thank you for a loving son – a son who lived life, made mistakes, made amends, and created unmistakable joy in our lives. Father, heal our hearts and comfort us in our tears – of sorrow and joy of a life gone too soon. Help us to remember his love in our laughter and our smiles. Thank you, Lord, for your strength. In Jesus' name we pray; be our strength.

Amen.

Pray, Journal, Reflect

_____

_____

_____

_____

_____

_____

_____

_____

_____

_____

Prayer of Comfort – Loss of a Daughter

My Lord, My God, we love you and give you glory, even as our hearts are heavy and hurt. We thank you for the years of life with our daughter. We thank you for her beauty and the purpose that she served. No longer with us, now with you, we cherish the memory, and we cherish the love. Father, give us comfort, hold our hands and hearts, we pray. Give us courage and strength to make it through this time. We need you, Lord, like never before. In Jesus' name we pray and lean on you.

Amen.

Pray, Journal, Reflect

_____

_____

_____

_____

_____

_____

_____

_____

_____

_____

Prayer of Comfort – Day of Passing

Father God, you came to bear all things. Father, we grieve today as we realize our loved one is no longer with us. We seek understanding and seek solace. Comfort our hearts; hear our prayer. We are breathless. Grant us strength. Thank you for listening. In Jesus' name we pray.

Amen.

Pray, Journal, Reflect

Prayer of Comfort – Day of the Service

My Lord, My God, thank you. Father, we come today to thank you for the years of love, laughter, and joy we shared with our mother. Thank you for her life, well-lived. Father, today we seek your comfort and your strength. We miss our mother, but we know that in You, she is well, better than she was here - and we are grateful - grateful for your love, your grace and your mercy. Be with us today as we lay her body to rest, but we know that her soul already rests with you. In Jesus' name we pray and say thank you.

Amen.

Pray, Journal, Reflect

_____

_____

_____

_____

_____

_____

_____

_____

_____

_____

Prayer of Comfort and Remembrance

Father, thank you for the years with both of our moms. Their love strengthened our lives and made us who we are. Thank you for the time they were here with us and as we celebrate this day and remember them both, we are sad, but we are grateful. Thank you for all things. Love and peace.

Amen.

Pray, Journal, Reflect

_____

_____

_____

_____

_____

_____

_____

_____

_____

_____

Vernet Clemons Nettles, Ed.D. |44

Prayer of Remembrance on Holidays

Gracious Father, thank you for all things - for every Easter program, Christmas Day, family dinner, and gathering we had with our mom, sister, aunt, cousin, friend. Help us to remember to enjoy this day and each day with love as she would have. Comfort us this holiday and all others. We love and miss her. In Jesus' name we pray for strength.

Amen.

Pray, Journal, Reflect

_____

_____

_____

_____

_____

_____

_____

_____

_____

_____

Prayer of Thanksgiving

Gracious Father, we thank you for all things and we thank you now for loving parents, who in their own way taught us to fight, to have strength, and to honor love. You have them there with you now but their love still reaches us here. We shall miss them terribly. As we feel their love around us, Father, send your Holy Spirit to comfort us and secure us in your mercy. We love you, Lord and we again say thank you for the treasured moments of family. In Jesus' name we pray.

Amen.

Pray, Journal, Reflect

_____

_____

_____

_____

_____

_____

_____

_____

_____

_____

Prayer of Comfort for Each Other

Glorious Father, we pray for ourselves as well for each other. Heal our hearts and hold us close. Give us comfort and strength as we move through this process. We thank you for the years of love and laughter with _____. We will miss _____ here, but we are joyful for the life you shared with us. Remind us that you love us, and you are here with us. Thank you, Lord, for all things. In Jesus' name we pray.

Amen.

"Trust in the Lord with all your heart, And lean not on your own understanding; In all your ways acknowledge Him, And He shall direct your paths."

Proverbs 3:5-6 NKJV

Prayer for Peace in Circumstances

Heavenly Father, thank you for all things. Bless us, Father, and cover us with your grace and mercy. Grant us peace knowing that you are with us and for us in all things. Grant us courage, Lord, to stand and to stay focused. Keep us and strengthen us, we pray in Jesus' name.

Amen.

Pray, Journal, Reflect

Prayer during the Unknown

Our Father, we ask for peace, strength, overflow, and courage as we participate in these tests and _____. We ask for healing and revelation through this process. Give the doctors answers so that we know which way to go from here. We love you and we thank you. In Jesus' name.

Amen

Pray, Journal, Reflect

_____

_____

_____

_____

_____

_____

_____

_____

_____

_____

Prayer in Preparation for Surgery

Good morning, Lord. As we approach the time of _____ 's surgery, we ask for calm and focus for her and her family as we prepare our hearts, homes, and minds. Give her focus to organize her home, her meals, her business, and her thoughts. Give her peace in her spirit that all will be well. Give her peace in her spirit that recovery will be well. And give her peace in her spirit that the next phase of life will be just as blessed and adventurous. In Jesus' name we pray and praise you in advance.

Amen.

Pray, Journal, Reflect

Prayer for Surgery

Our Lord Our God, thank you for blessings beyond measure. We pray for comfort and calm. We pray that you bless this surgery and its outcome for our friend. Guide the hands and wisdom of the surgeon and the medical staff. Surround _____ with your loving care, your peace, and your healing power. We love our friend, and we love you, Lord. We thank you in advance for your loving kindness and your grace. For these things we pray and praise in Jesus' name.

Amen.

Pray, Journal, Reflect

_____

_____

_____

_____

_____

_____

_____

_____

_____

_____

_____

Prayer for Healing

Heavenly Father, thank you for bringing such a wonderful person and beautiful spirit into our lives. We thank you for every opportunity we continue to have and have had to share and show love to _____ and their family.

We thank you for _____'s love and kindness. Father, we continue to lift _____ in prayer. We pray for comfort and your miraculous healing power. You are an ever present and all-knowing healer. We love you and we thank you in advance for your comfort, your presence, and your power. In Jesus' name we pray and seek your strength.

Amen.

Pray, Journal, Reflect

_____

_____

_____

_____

_____

_____

_____

_____

_____

_____

Prayer for Healing

Heavenly Father, thank you for all things. We pray your will, Father, and your healing touch and grace. We seek rest and peace in your embrace. Encircle us, Father, so that we may feel you and your strength in the midst of this time. We pray for this and other blessings. In Jesus' name.

Amen

"Now He who searches the hearts knows what the mind of the Spirit is, because He makes intercession for the saints according to the will of God."

Romans 8:27 NKJV

Prayer of Thanksgiving

Glory Hallelujah Father, we thank you that you are a sovereign Lord. Thank you for having order in all things - even when we feel like we are spinning out of control, you are in control. Thank you for reminding us to trust, for reminding us to stay focused on you, even though we may feel barren or lost. Remind us that you have control of all things. And when it is our season, Father, our purpose will manifest, just as you have promised. In Jesus' name we pray. Yes, Lord.

Amen.

Pray, Journal, Reflect

_____

_____

_____

_____

_____

_____

_____

_____

_____

_____

Prayer for our Church

Heavenly Father, as we prepare for another year in our church, we are humbled at your grace and favor, for you have brought this congregation from a mighty long way. And in bringing us forward this year, carrying our burdens, and blessing us through all struggles, we are aware that you have something more for us. Speak Lord, into this congregation and into us individually and into our families so that we may be and do what you would have. In Jesus' name we pray.

Amen.

Pray, Journal, Reflect

_____

_____

_____

_____

_____

_____

_____

_____

_____

_____

_____

Prayer for Ministry

Heavenly Father, thank you for all things. Father, thank you for this opportunity to serve in this ministry. Thank you for the opportunity to serve with others who are of like mind and who believe in service to others. Thank you, indeed, for our Chair, who has heard and seen your vision of service to those in need. We come to you collectively to see clearly the foundation that you would like for us to build.

Guide us to understanding - so that we are all clear of our focus. Guide us to community - so that we are all working in one accord. Guide us to resources - so that we know where and how to frame and build this service. Guide us to patience - so that we can work and wait patiently as you reveal each movement to us in Your time.

Also, Father, guide us to peace - so that we continue to work on one accord with each other. You have given the Chair the vision, and us the hands, legs, and feet. Guide us, we pray. We are listening. In Jesus' name we pray.

Amen.

Pray, Journal, Reflect

_____

_____

_____

_____

_____

_____

_____

_____

_____

_____

Pray, Journal, Reflect

Prayer for Guidance

Heavenly Father, pull my anger and disappointment from me so that I may do and be what you would have me to be – a _____ and a laborer for you and your glory. Not about me Father, but all about you. In Jesus' name I seek you and pray.

Amen.

Pray, Journal, Reflect

_____

_____

_____

_____

_____

_____

_____

_____

_____

_____

Prayer to Ease our Fears

My Lord, my Father, cover my friend and ease her fears. She knows you and knows that you are always with her. Cover her and cover her husband. Remind her and us that Faith is our normal. We love you and ask for your peace. Father, we also ask for courage and peace and knowledge for our health care providers. Give them the knowledge and courage to guide us and serve us. For this and many other blessings we pray and praise you in advance.

Amen.

Pray, Journal, Reflect

_____

_____

_____

_____

_____

_____

_____

_____

_____

_____

_____

Vernet Clemons Nettles, Ed.D. |74

Prayer for Marriage

Gracious Father, thank you. Thank you for my spouse – my _____. Thank you for our love, our life, and our courage to see and know each other. Father, we love each other, but we are stumbling. Remind us, Lord, that this is not the end, it is an episode in the love story that you have written for us. Help us to know that even in this scene you are with us. Give us the courage to allow this space in our lives to grow us closer to you and closer to each other. Lord, we do not want to give up. Keep us as we relearn to keep each other. In Jesus' name we pray and praise you in advance.

Amen.

Pray, Journal, Reflect

_____

_____

_____

_____

_____

_____

_____

_____

_____

_____

Prayer for Teachers during a Pandemic

Heavenly Father, we come today in praise and thanksgiving for all that you do and have done for us. We thank you for your grace and mercy during this pandemic and especially during this time of learning and relearning. Father, we pray today for our teachers. Our teachers in the buildings and our teachers in the homes.

Father, we ask for guidance, patience, and creativity as we learn to serve our students in different, yet still meaningful ways. Grant us comfort, allow us to see the other side of the struggle, so we know that we will and have become better servants to our students and to you.

And for our mom-teachers at home, grant them patience and understanding. Pour into them comfort so that they can in-turn ease the anxiety of their children-students. Show them as well that we will all have learned more about ourselves and will draw closer to you before this is over.

Remind us, Lord, that we are all servants, that we serve one another so that we all can move forward together. Keep us strong; keep us encouraged; keep us close. Remind us that we truly are in this together, and with your love and covering we will make it through - wiser, stronger, and together. In Jesus' name we pray and praise you in advance. Thank you, Lord.

Amen.

Pray, Journal, Reflect

_____

_____

_____

_____

_____

_____

_____

_____

_____

_____

Pray, Journal, Reflect

_____

_____

_____

_____

_____

_____

_____

_____

_____

_____

Vernet Clemons Nettles, Ed.D. |80

Prayer for Peace during a Pandemic

My Lord, My God, we come to you exhausted, concerned, and confused. Father, we are doing all that we can - please continue to give us strength, comfort, and peace as we move through another round of this virus. Father, please watch over my family. Be our immune system boosters. In Jesus' name we pray and rest.

Amen.

Pray, Journal, Reflect

Vernet Clemons Nettles, Ed.D. |82

Prayer for Patience during a Pandemic

My Lord, My God, Good Morning. We come to you this morning with praise and thanksgiving. Thank you for this opportunity to serve the children and teachers in our school system. We pray today for courage and strength. Courage to do what you have called us to do with the gifts and talents you have given. We pray for strength to weather the rain and sometimes storms of jealousy, obstinance, and disregard of others. Give us the words and wisdom to respond with grace or not respond at all. Give us understanding, I pray. Pour into us, Father, your spirit, and your joy so that it is a part of who we are. Thank you, Lord, for these thy gifts. In Jesus' name we pray and praise.

Amen.

Pray, Journal, Reflect

_____

_____

_____

_____

_____

_____

_____

_____

_____

_____

Vernet Clemons Nettles, Ed.D. |84

"Now it came to pass, as He was praying in a certain place, when He ceased, that one of His disciples said to Him, "Lord, teach us to pray, as John also taught his disciples.""

Luke 11:1 NKJV

(Luke 11:2-4 NKJV)

"Therefore do not be like them. For your Father knows the things you have need of before you ask Him."

Matthew 6:8 NKJV

(Matthew 6:9-13 NKJV)

Pray, Journal, Reflect

_____

_____

_____

_____

_____

_____

_____

_____

_____

_____

Vernet Clemons Nettles, Ed.D. |86

The Lord's Prayer

"In this manner, therefore, pray: Our Father in heaven, Hallowed be Your name.

Your kingdom come. Your will be done On earth as it is in heaven.

Give us this day our daily bread.

And forgive us our debts, As we forgive our debtors.

And do not lead us into temptation, But deliver us from the evil one. For Yours is the kingdom and the power and the glory forever. ***Amen.***"

Matthew 6:9-13 NKJV

Pray, Journal, Reflect

Vernet Clemons Nettles, Ed.D. |88

Pray, Journal, Reflect

Pray, Journal, Reflect

_____

_____

_____

_____

_____

_____

_____

_____

_____

_____

_____

Vernet Clemons Nettles, Ed.D. |90

Scripture Index

Old Testament

New Testament

Vernet Clemons Nettles, Ed.D. |92

Bibliography

https://www.kremp.com/etymology-and-symbolism-of-50-flowers

(This is not an endorsement of Kremp Florists. This is simply an acknowledgement of the origin of the information used.)

Vernet Clemons Nettles, Ed.D. |94

About the Author

Vernet Clemons Nettles, EdD is a parent, educator, and poet. She resides in Montgomery, AL, where she has served as a Christian educator in her church Hutchinson Missionary Baptist and currently serves as an Education Specialist in the Montgomery Public Schools.

Since 2014, she has shared daily prayers on her website: Another Day's Journey. To connect with Vernet, visit http://www.vcndailypray.com or http://www.vernetcnettles.com

Social Media
Facebook: @vernet.nettles

Vernet Clemons Nettles, Ed.D. |96

Author's Works

Why Should I Be Bound? Musings on a Journey with God (2018)

Why Should I Be Bound? Musings on a Journey with God (2018) – Large Print Edition

Moments of Grace – A 2020 Devotional Planner (7 x 10 & 8.5 x 11) (2019)

UnSpoken Words – A Poetry Collection (2020)

Pray, Praise and Be Encouraged – A 21 day devotional (2020)

Walking With Grace – A 2021 Devotional Planner (2020)

Vernet Clemons Nettles, Ed.D. |98

Made in the USA
Columbia, SC
29 December 2021

51535122R00063